HEAR
MY CRY

HEAR MY CRY

A daily prayer book for Advent

Ruth Burgess

WILD GOOSE PUBLICATIONS

www.ionabooks.com

Published by
Wild Goose Publications
4th Floor, Savoy House, 140 Sauchiehall St, Glasgow G2 3DH, UK
web: www.ionabooks.com
Wild Goose Publications is the publishing division of the Iona Community. Scottish
Charity No. SCO03794. Limited Company Reg. No. SCO96243.

ISBN 1 901557 95 2

Cover illustration © Scott Riley

A catalogue record for this book is available from the British Library.

Overseas distribution
Australia: Willow Connection Pty Ltd, Unit 4A, 3-9 Kenneth Road,
Manly Vale, NSW 2093
New Zealand: Pleroma, Higginson Street, Otane 4170,
Central Hawkes Bay
Canada: Bayard Distribution, 49 Front Street East, Toronto, Ontario M5E 1B3

Permission to reproduce any part of this work in Australia or New Zealand should be
sought from Willow Connection.

Printed by Bell & Bain, Thornliebank, Glasgow, UK

CONTENTS

For Pam – old friend
with love

INTRODUCTION

The Advent antiphons – 'The Great O's'– have been sung in the Church's liturgy during the last week of Advent, possibly since the seventh century. From the winter depths of our waiting and longing for the light, the cries of Advent recall our experience of what God is like and call on God to come to our aid.

The season of Advent creates a space where people are encouraged to sit still and to explore the darkness of their own vulnerability – a space to ask questions, a space to wonder, a space to touch home.

By using the antiphons we invite God to come and show us what we need to know. We ask God to stretch out a hand to us, to comfort us, to disturb us, to lead us into light and truth.

We are aware that encountering truth – especially truth about ourselves – is not easy. We know that God's coming will not leave us the same as before. We need the message of the angels – 'Be not afraid' – to encourage us to invite God to meet us and save us and set us free.

The short days and long winter nights are full of cries.

I have enjoyed putting this book together. I am greatly indebted to Lynda Wright for helpful comments and suggestions relating to reflective prayer and to Jane Darroch-Riley for her artwork. My thanks, too, as always, to the team at Wild Goose Publications: Sandra, Neil, Jane, Tri and Alex, for their encouragement and support.

DAILY READINGS – SUGGESTIONS FOR USE

Traditionally, the Advent antiphons are sung from the 17th to the 23rd of December. The material in this book takes the antiphons as a pattern for prayer, reflection and action throughout Advent.

We pray in many ways – in silence, song and speech, with our imaginations, in our actions. Not all our days are the same; sometimes our prayer feels like a hard struggle, at other times it fills us with wonder and delight. There are days when we can choose a place and time to pray; on other days we pray as and when we are able.

When we pray we consciously bring ourselves and our world into God's presence. No part of our world or ourselves is outside of God's concern and love. Our prayer involves the whole of who we are.

Some of the suggestions in this book may not seem like 'prayer' to you, but all of them are offered as ways of coming close to God. Some prayers may 'work' for you, others may not, but I invite you to wait and listen, to taste and touch and see. On some days there are a number of suggestions for prayer. You might choose one or try them all!

The format for each day's prayer is the same:

☆ Bible verse

☆ Advent cry

☆ Suggestion/s for prayer

Some ways to use this material

☆ Read the Bible verse and Advent cry early in the day. If a particular word or phrase speaks to you, carry it with you into the day; repeat it to yourself in time with your breath; write it down somewhere – on the fridge door, on your misted windscreen, in your diary. Let it become part of you. Let God speak to you through it. During the day or evening follow the suggestion for prayer.

☆ Read the Bible verse and Advent cry. Reflect on what it brings to mind – a Bible story, an encounter with God in your own life, a face you have seen in the street or in the news. Create your own prayer, reflection or meditation.

☆ Read the Bible verse and the Advent cry. Reflect on what it brings to mind (see above). Add colour to the line drawing of the candle on the page (use watercolours, coloured pencils – buy some new ones for Advent). Choose colours that reflect your thoughts and prayers.

☆ Read the Bible verse and the Advent cry and follow the suggestion for prayer. Add your own pictures to the blank spaces on the page. Draw pictures. Use illustrations from newspapers and magazines, photographs, postcards, copies of paintings and sculpture. Make a collage.

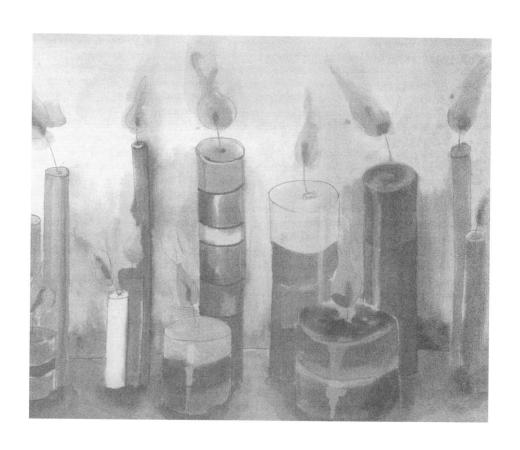

DAILY READINGS & PRAYERS

27th November – 24th December

27TH NOVEMBER

Do not be afraid – I am with you!
From the distant east and the farthest west,
I will bring my people home.
Isaiah 43:5

O Gatherer,
seeking Your people in the cities and the wilderness:
Come put Your arms around us
and bring us safely home.

Where have you experienced home?
Think about what home means for you.

Imagine yourself being at home
in the loving arms of God.
Relax and feel secure.

28TH NOVEMBER

A voice cries out,
'Prepare in the wilderness
a road for God.'
Isaiah 40:3

O Disturber,
herald of life and change:
Come drag us from our safe havens
and plant our feet on the road of life.

Is there anything in your preparations for Christmas
that you want or need to change?

Try to be still today for a few moments.
Prepare a place within you to hear God's voice.

29TH NOVEMBER

The desert will rejoice,
and flowers will blossom in the wilderness.
The desert will sing and shout for joy.
Isaiah 35:1

O Flower of Jesse's stem,
blooming in places that no one expected:
Come sow Your seeds in us
and bring them to beauty and blossom.

Use a flower as a focus for your prayers.
Look at it. Smell it. Enjoy its fragile beauty.

30TH NOVEMBER

Andrew said, 'There is a boy here
who has five loaves of barley bread
and two fish.'
John 6:8

O Bread of Life,

You welcome a man's trust and a child's gift:

Come, use what we have

to feed those who are hungry.

Slowly eat a piece of bread. Taste its goodness.
Reflect on your need to be nourished.

If you are able, go without a meal today
and give to charity.

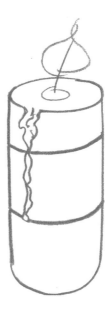

1ˢᵗ DECEMBER

I call you friends,
because I have told you everything
I have heard from God.
John15:15

O Friend,
always wanting the best for us,
trusting us with justice and love:
Come walk beside us
and share our joys and fears.

Pray for your friends, past and present.

If you can, spend time with a friend today.

Write Jesus a friendly letter.
Share your news and plans.

2ND DECEMBER

He will come to judge
like one who refines and purifies silver.
Malachi 3:3

O Refiner,
Sifter, Separator, Smelter:
Come burn up the dross in us
and mark us with love.

What are the marks of God's presence in your life?

Use a piece of hallmarked metal
(a spoon, a bowl, a cross)
as a focus for your prayers.

3RD DECEMBER

The Kingdom of heaven is like this:
A man happens to find a treasure hidden in a field …
Matthew 13:44

O Treasure,
dandelion in the concrete,
gold in the field:
Come and call us to search for You
in the waste places of our world.

Go for a walk.
Use your senses to let God speak to you
from the things around you.

Reflect on where you find God
and where God finds you.

4TH DECEMBER

When it was time for the feast,
he sent his servants to tell his guests,
'Come, all is ready.'
Luke 14:17

O Party Giver,
brooker of no excuses:
Come send Your saints to find us
and compel us to the feast.

Reflect on what excuses you usually use.

Ask God to surprise you today.
Accept the gifts that you are offered.
Say thank you.

5TH DECEMBER

I am surrounded by many troubles –
too many to count!
My sins have caught up with me
and I can no longer see;
they are more than the hairs of my head,
and I have lost my courage.
Save me, Lord! Help me now!
Psalm 40:12,13

O God,

You love me:

Come,

come quickly.

I need Your help.

Sit quietly. Let your own need surface.

Stretch out your hands and ask for the help you need.

Pray for someone who needs God's help today.

6ᵀᴴ DECEMBER

Wake up, my soul.
Wake up, my harp, my lyre:
I will wake up the sun.
Psalm 108:1,2

O Quickener,
energy of the universe:
Come waken us
and fill us with love and life.

Play and/or sing a song that wakes you up.
Dance if you want to.

Try to watch the sun rise today (or tomorrow).

7TH DECEMBER

When they ask me, what is your name,
what can I tell them?
Exodus 3:13,14

O God of the burning bush,

You are who You are,

You will be who You will be:

Come and summon us onto holy ground.

What names do you call God?

Take off your shoes.

Feel the ground under your feet.

Appreciate that you are standing on holy ground.

8TH DECEMBER

You are in my hands,
just like clay in the potter's hands.
Jeremiah 18:5

O Potter,
pummeller and moulder of clay:
Come make of us something useful for Your world.

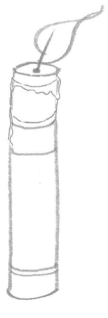

Be creative.
Make or mend something with your hands today.

Use your imagination.
Picture the 'pot' which is you –
the creation that God the potter
has made for the world.

9TH DECEMBER

God is near all those who call.
God hears our cries.
Psalm 145:18,19

O Child of the manger,
totally dependent on Joseph and Mary:
Come and show us our own vulnerability,
our need for hugs and smiles.

Reflect on your own vulnerability.

Try to give and receive a hug/lots of hugs today.

10TH DECEMBER

Jesus wept.
John 11:35

O Weeper,
You cried at the grave of Your friend:
Come and put Your arms
around those who mourn and miss the people they love.

Look at some photos of those you miss and love.
Imagine yourself and Jesus wiping away each other's tears.

Pray for those who mourn.

11TH DECEMBER

The people asked John,
'What are we to do?'
He answered,
'Whoever has two shirts must give one to the person who has none;
whoever has food must share it.'
Luke 3:10,11

O Baptiser,
just and bright and full of glory:
Come bring us to repentance
and turn us round to face You;
plunge us deep into justice and truth.

What could you give away?

12TH DECEMBER

Give strength to hands that are tired
and to knees that tremble with weakness.
Isaiah 35:3

O Lover of the little ones,
their guardian and defender:
Come with Your angels and cradle Your children,
and guide their stumbling feet along the homeward road.

Be in touch with your own tiredness.
Try to breathe in the energy of God.

Pray for the little ones in your community.
Pray for those who stumble.

13TH DECEMBER

There is the ocean large and wide
and in it plays Leviathan,
the sea monster you made to amuse you.
Psalm 104:26

O Maker of laughter,
who plays with Leviathan in the deep waters:
Come stretch out Your hands
to cuddle and tickle Your children
through the moments of their days.

Spend time playing today,
doing something you really enjoy.

14TH DECEMBER

God said,
'We will make human beings;
they will be like us and resemble us.'
Genesis 1:26

O loving Mother,
whose presence offends many
and delights many more:
Come and help us to see clearly
the One in whose likeness we are made
and rejoice.

Reflect on the motherhood and fatherhood of God.

Look in a mirror and smile.

15TH DECEMBER

Those who trust God for help
will find their strength renewed;
they will rise on wings like eagles.
Isaiah 40:31

O Pilgrim God,
abandoning that which is no longer needed:
Come with us on our journey;
show us how to travel lightly,
keeping only what we need to grow.

How lightly do you travel?

Are you carrying something in particular
that you need to trust into God's hands?

16TH DECEMBER

Evil people make slaves of orphans
and take children in payment for debts.
The poor go out with no clothes to protect them.
They go hungry whilst harvesting wheat.
In the cities the wounded and dying cry out,
but God ignores their prayers.
Job 24:9–12

O Listener,
You hear our howls of anger and protest,
our righteous cries:
Come with glory and integrity.
Work Your justice through our lives.

Read today's newspaper.
Pray for those who are wronged and in need –
those living under the burden of third world debt,
those falsely imprisoned …

Bring the energy of your righteous anger to God:
speak or shout your concerns and questions,
write to your local councillor or Member of Parliament,
go for a run, clean the windows, dig the garden …
When you are exhausted, rest.
Imagine yourself held in God's arms.

17TH DECEMBER

Wisdom is a breath of God's power;
a pure and radiant stream of glory from the Almighty.
Wisdom of Solomon 7:25

O Wisdom,
wiser than our foolishness,
holier than our sin:
Come, blow us clean,
and bring us to God.

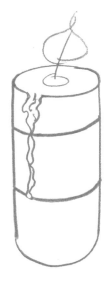

Where in your life do you most feel in need
of God's wisdom?

Go for a walk in the wind or fly a kite.

Breathe in deeply.
Let God's wisdom and glory fill your life
and blow the dust out of your dark corners.

18TH DECEMBER

Do for others
what you want them to do for you.
This is the meaning of the law of Moses
and the teaching of the prophets.
Matthew 7:12

O Ruler of Israel,
You speak through Your prophets;
Your words hold us and challenge us and keep us right:
Come and tell us the truths that we need to know
and write them into our hearts and lives.

What truths do you live by?

What do you want for yourself?

19TH DECEMBER

Just as new branches grow from a tree stump,
so a new king will rise from David's descendants.
He will rule his people with justice and integrity.
Isaiah 11:1,5

O Root of Jesse, Lion of Judah,
the wisdom and integrity of God is in You:
Come and seek us out
and root Your justice in us.

Walk among trees.
Imagine their roots under your feet.

Use a leaf or a bare twig as a focus
for your prayers.

Where are your roots,
your sources of nourishment?

20TH DECEMBER

Jesus said,
'I am the gate.
Whoever comes in by me will be saved,
and will come in and go out
and find pasture.
John 10: 9

O Key of David,
opening the doors to hope and heaven:
Come, walk with us through the darkness
and bring us safe over the threshold
into life and light.

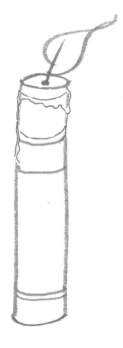

What doors have opened or shut for you this year?

What doors would you like to open, or to firmly close?

Use a key as a focus for your prayers,
or stand in a doorway as you pray.

21ˢᵀ DECEMBER

I, Jesus, am descended from the family of David;
I am the bright morning star.
Revelation 22:16

O Sun of Justice,
O Bright Morning Star,
herald of light and joy:
Come, shine in our darkness and bring us hope.

Light a candle in a dark room.
Focus on your breathing.
Breathe in God's light, let it dance inside you.
Breathe out and let go of your anxiety, doubt and fear.

Spend time looking at the sky and the stars.

22ND DECEMBER

Praise God;
hills and mountains,
animals tame and wild,
kings and all peoples,
princes and all other rulers,
young women and young men,
old people and children too.
Psalm 148:10,11

O King of the peoples,
You cherish and love all Your creation,
You long for the nations to be at peace:
Come, help us to love and care for Your world.

Watch the news
and pray for those who are happy.
Pray for rulers and world leaders.
Pray for those who are in trouble
or in need.

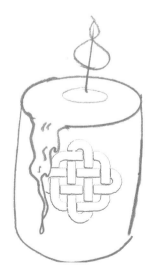

23ʳᵈ DECEMBER

A woman who is pregnant will have a son
and name him Emmanuel,
which means 'God is with us'.
Isaiah 7:14

O Emmanuel,

God among us, beside us, within us:

Come into our communities, our homes, our lives.

Come quickly, and stay.

Reflect on signs of God's presence
in your community.

In time with your breath,
pray *Maranatha, Come Lord Jesus.*

24TH DECEMBER

During the day try to spend a few minutes in prayer.

Choose one of your Christmas cards as a focus for your prayers.

Sit quietly. Light a candle. Wonder at the mystery of God.

You will find a baby
wrapped in strips of cloth
and lying in a manger.
Luke 2:12

O baby Jesus,
alive and vulnerable in our world,
more like us than we could have ever imagined:
The waiting is over,
God is here.

Sing your favourite Christmas carol
before you go to bed tonight.

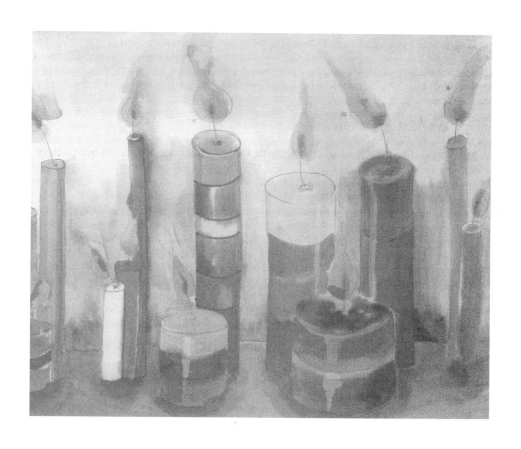

THE CRIES OF ADVENT –
background information

THE CRIES OF ADVENT –
BACKGROUND INFORMATION

The Concise Oxford Dictionary defines an antiphon as:

Noun: 1. a hymn or psalm, the parts of which are sung or recited alternately by two groups.
       2. a versicle or phrase from this.
       3. a sentence sung or recited before or after a psalm or canticle.

The seven Advent antiphons (sometimes known as 'The Great O's') are traditionally sung at vespers or evening prayer from the 17th to the 23rd of December. They are sung before and after the Magnificat (Luke 1:46–55). The Advent antiphons are based on scriptural references to the coming of the Messiah (see pages 57–71). Through the titles of the antiphons, the action of God in history is traced from the presence of Wisdom with God before creation to the coming of God in Jesus at Bethlehem. The seven antiphons begin

O Wisdom,
O Ruler of the House of Israel,
O Root of Jesse,
O Key of David,
O Rising Dawn,
O King of the Gentiles,
O Emmanuel.

Many Christians are familiar with five of the Advent antiphons from the hymn 'O Come, O Come, Emmanuel' (1851). John Mason Neale, an Anglican clergyman, translated this song from a medieval Latin hymn. There have been other translations by Thomas Alexander Lacey (1801–1931), John Henry Newman (1801–1890) and Henry Sloane Coffin (1877–1954). The translation by Thomas Lacey is included in *The English Hymnal* of 1906.

There is an eighth-century Anglo-Saxon poem known as 'The Advent Lyrics' which is based on the antiphons. This may have been written by Cynewulf, Bishop of Lindisfarne, and is found in *The Exeter Book*, a manuscript that has belonged to the chapter library of Exeter Cathedral since 1072. Charles W. Kennedy, a translator of the antiphons, wrote of The Advent Lyrics: 'They combine a poet's skill and a churchman's religious feeling. They clothe with lyric grace the meditations of a devout Christian deeply moved by the spirit of Advent, and trained in the significance of its mysteries.'[1] The Advent Lyrics add four 'lesser' antiphons to the seven 'great' antiphons. These are O Virgin of Virgins, O Mistress of the World, O Jerusalem and O Prince of Peace.

There may have been a monastic tradition that on the night of the 17th of December, the abbot would sing the first antiphon and on succeeding nights other principal monks would take their turns. After the evening service, the monk who had sung the antiphon was expected to provide a treat, usually edible, for the other monks.

[1] *Early English Christian Poetry*, edited by Charles W. Kennedy, translated by Charles W. Kennedy, copyright © 1963 by Oxford University Press, Inc.

Bibliography and websites

An Anthology of Old English Poetry, translated by Charles W. Kennedy, New York, Oxford University Press, 1960.

Early English Christian Poetry, edited by Charles W. Kennedy, translated by Charles W. Kennedy, copyright © 1963 by Oxford University Press, Inc.

The antiphons of Advent, Jeanne Kun www.rc.net/wcc/antiphon.htm

The English Hymnal, Oxford University Press, 1906.

The Promise of His Glory: services and prayers for the season, from All Saints to Candlemas, Church House Publishers/Mowbray, 1991, ISBN 0715137387.

www.hymnsandcarolsofchristmas.com

www.yorku.ca/inpar/Christ_Kennedy.pdf

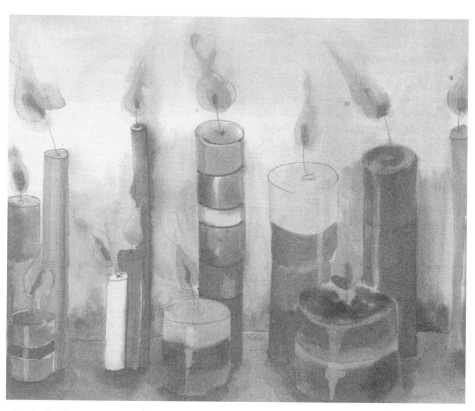

BIBLICAL & LITERARY REFERENCES

for the Advent antiphons

17th December

SAPENTIA – WISDOM

Prayer

O Wisdom, breath of God's power,
Your glory fills the streets and skies,
You order all things sweetly and justly:
Come, blow us clean
and teach us wonder and truth.

Biblical references

Proverbs 1:20
Listen, Wisdom is calling out in the streets and market places.

Isaiah 11:2,3
The Spirit of the Lord will give him wisdom,
and the knowledge and skill to rule his people …
He will not judge by appearance or hearsay;
he will judge the poor fairly
and defend the rights of the helpless.

Wisdom of Solomon 7:25
Wisdom is a breath of God's power,
a pure and radiant stream of glory from the Almighty.

Sirach (Ecclesiasticus) 24:3
I am the word spoken by the most high.
I covered the earth like a mist.

Sirach 24:9
My Creator created me in eternity, before time began,
and I will exist for all eternity to come.

I Corinthians 1:25
What seems to be God's foolishness is wiser than human wisdom,
and what seems to be God's weakness is stronger than human strength.

From the Advent antiphons

Thou art the wisdom   that, with the All-Wielder,
This wide Creation   fashioned of old.[1]

Wise it is for all men   who have remembrance
Most often, and most sincerely,   and with most zeal
To glorify God.

---

[1] All the Advent antiphons in this section are from the book *Early English Christian Poetry*, edited by Charles W. Kennedy, translated by Charles W. Kennedy, copyright © 1963 by Oxford University Press, Inc. Used by permission of Oxford University Press, Inc. (The original Advent antiphons are attributed to Cynewulf, Bishop of Lindisfarne, eighth century.)

18th December

ADONAI – RULER

Prayer

O God and Ruler of Israel,
who appeared as a burning flame
and rescued Your people:
Come, stretch out Your arms
and save us.

Biblical references

Exodus 3:2
The Angel of the Lord appeared to Moses as a flame coming from the middle
of a bush.

Exodus 6:6
Tell the Israelites that I say to them,
'I will rescue you and set you free;
I will raise my arm to save you.'

Isaiah 11:5
He will rule his people with justice and integrity.

Micah 5:2

The Lord says, 'Bethlehem, you are one of the smallest towns in Judah,
but out of you I will bring a ruler for Israel,
whose family line goes back to ancient times.'

From the Advent antiphons

Now is the babe come   born to transform
The works of the Hebrews.   He brings thee bliss,
Looses thy bondage,   draws nigh unto men,
For He only knows   their harrowing need,
How man in his wretchedness   waits upon mercy.

19th December

RADIX – ROOT

Prayer

O Root of Jesse,
before whom all kings will keep silence,
and whose story all people will hear:
Come quickly and save us.
Come soon.

Biblical references

Isaiah 9:6,7
A child is born to us.
A son is given to us.
He will rule as King David's successor,
basing his power on right and justice,
from now until the end of time.

Isaiah 11:1
The royal line of David is like a tree that has been cut down;
but just as new branches sprout from a stump,
so a new king will arise from among David's descendants.

Isaiah 11:10

A day is coming when the new king from the royal throne of David will be a symbol to the nations. They will gather in his royal city and give him honour.

Isaiah 53:2

It was the will of the Lord that his servant should grow like a plant taking root in dry ground.

Luke 1:32,33

The Lord God will make him a king, as his ancestor David was, and he will be the king of the descendants of Jacob for ever; his kingdom will never end.

From the Advent Antiphons

the King of glory
Himself approaches   to seek thee out,
To abide in thee,   as the blessed prophets
In their books foretold   the birth of the Christ,
To thy comfort spoke,   thou fairest of cities!

20th December

CLAVIS – KEY

Prayer

O Key of David,
opener and closer of locks and doors:
Come, free us from the chains of misery and injustice
and destroy the darkness of death.

Biblical references

Isaiah 22:22
I will give him complete authority under the king, the descendant of David. He will have the keys of office; what he opens, no one will shut, and what he shuts, no one will open.

Isaiah 42:6,7
I, the Lord, have called you and given you power to see that justice is done on earth. Through you I will make a covenant with all peoples; through you I will bring light to the nations. You will open the eyes of the blind and set free those who sit in dark prisons.

Revelation 3:7

He has the key that belonged to David, and when he opens a door, no one can close it, and when he closes it, no one can open it.

From the Advent antiphons

O Thou Ruler   and Righteous King,
Keeping the keys,   unlocking life,
Grant us salvation

Bless earth with thine advent,   O Saviour Christ,
And the golden gates   which in days gone by
Full long stood locked,   High Lord of Heaven,
Bid Thou swing open   and seek us out
Humbly descending   to the hordes of earth.

21st December

ORIENS – RISING DAWN

Prayer

O Morning Star,
Sun of Justice, Righteous Healer:
Come, shine in the darkness
and bring us light.

Biblical references

Isaiah 9:2
The people who walked in darkness have seen a great light.
They lived in a land of shadows, but now light is shining on them.

Malachi 4:2
My saving power will rise on you like the sun
and bring healing like the sun's rays.

Luke 1:78,79
Our God is merciful and tender.
He will cause the bright dawn of salvation to rise on us
and to shine from heaven
on all those who live in the dark shadow of death,
to guide our steps into the path of peace.

2 Peter 1:19

We are even more confident of the message proclaimed by the prophets. You will do well to pay attention to it, because it is like a lamp shining in a dark place until the day dawns and the light of the morning star shines in your hearts.

Revelation 22:16

I am descended from the family of David;
I am the bright morning star.

From the Advent antiphons

O Rising Sun!   Most radiant angel
Over the middle-earth   sent unto men!
Thou steadfast glow   and gleaming of the sun
Bright beyond stars!

                    come Thyself
To illumine those   who have long been sitting
Attired with darkness   in eternal night …

22nd December

REX – KING

Prayer

O King of the peoples,
cornerstone binding nations together,
You fashioned us all out of dust:
Come and fit us together
into Your building.

Biblical references

Isaiah 28:16
I am placing in Zion a foundation that is firm and strong. In it I am putting a solid cornerstone on which are written the words, 'Faith that is firm is also patient.'

Jeremiah 10:7
Who would not honour you, the King of all nations?
You deserve to be honoured.

Psalm 118:22 / Matthew 21:42
The stone which the builders rejected as worthless
has turned out to be the most important of all.

Ephesians 2:14

Christ himself has brought us peace by making Jews and Gentiles one people.

From the Advent antiphons

Thou art the wall-stone   the workers rejected
Of old from the work.   It befits Thee well
That Thou shouldst be Head   of the glorious hall
Locking together   the lengthy walls,
The flint unbroken,   in a firm embrace,
That ever on earth   the eyes of all
May look with wonder   on the Lord of glory.

December 23rd

EMMANUEL – GOD WITH US

Prayer

O Emmanuel,
King and Protector,
saviour of all people:
Come among us
and set us free.

Biblical references

Isaiah 7:14
The Lord himself will give you a sign:
a young woman who is pregnant will have a son
and will name him Emmanuel.

Isaiah 8:8
God is with us!
His outspread wings protect everything.

Isaiah 33:22
The Lord himself will be our King;
He will rule over us and protect us.

Matthew 1:23

Now all this happened in order to make what the Lord had said through the prophet come true, 'A virgin will become pregnant and have a son, and he will be called Emmanuel, which means, "God is with us".'

From the Advent antiphons

The maid was young,   the Immaculate Virgin,
Whom He chose as Mother;   without man's love
The Bride grew great   with the Son's conception.
Never in all the world   early or late
Was woman's conceiving   such as this.
It was a marvellous mystery   of God!

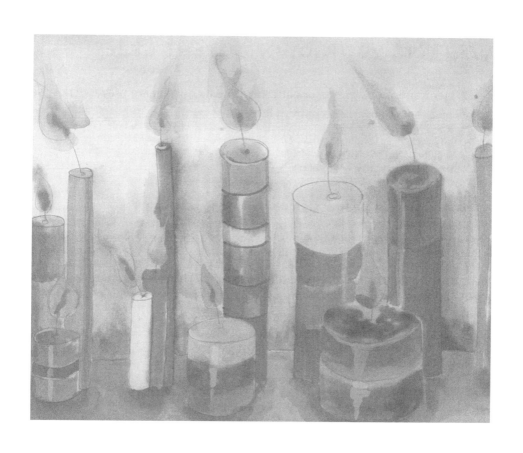

WRITING YOUR OWN
ADVENT CRIES

WRITING YOUR OWN ADVENT CRIES

The Advent antiphons give us a pattern with which to create prayers/cries for others and for ourselves. The pattern is clear:

☆ O
☆ A title of God or the Messiah
☆ An attribute of God suggested by the title
☆ An invitation to God to act, preceded by the word 'Come'.

The cry is based on the title chosen, and uses imagery relating to it. For example, if the title chosen is 'Shepherd', relevant Bible passages might be 'He leads me to quiet pools of fresh water' (Psalm 23:2), or 'He calls his own sheep by name and he leads them out' (John 10:3).

The cry could then be developed:

☆ O
☆ Shepherd
☆ You know your sheep by name
☆ Come and lead us into safe pasture.

Titles/names for God can be found throughout scripture. Looking at the same passage in different versions of the scriptures can be helpful. A Bible concordance can be useful too. Other sources of names and titles include hymns and songs and collections of prayers, old and new. Music, art and literature, the media, nature and the holy writings of all religious faiths can also be sources of inspiration.

After you have decided on the title/name of God you want to use in your prayer, you may find it helpful to bring your research about the name together, and look at it all again before you begin to write. You might find it refreshing to take a break between research and writing. You may want to jot down ideas and write your prayer over a few days.

For a number of years I have kept, in a notebook, a list of the different titles/names for God (Father, Son and Holy Spirit) that I have discovered. I find this list very useful when writing prayers and liturgy.

Here are some names from my notebook, with spaces to add your own favourite names and discoveries.

Enjoy your research and writing.

TITLES/NAMES FOR GOD
– the beginnings of a list

Alpha and Omega
Almighty
All merciful

Bread of life
Bright flame
Breath of the universe

Crying God
Comforter
Challenger
Chief of chiefs
Child of the manger

Dancer
Dreamer
Disturber
Destroyer of darkness
Defender

Elemental God
Encircler

Fire of fires
Friend of sinners
First and last
Forgiver

Giver of growth
Great God
Green, gardener God
Guardian of the little ones
Gatherer

Holy
Healer
Highway home
Heir of all things

Immediate
Intimate

Joy of joys
Justice maker

Keeper

Lightener of the stars
Living stream
Lion of Judah
Lamb of God
Liberator

Mystery maker
Midwife
Mouth of mercy

Nourisher

Open-handed God

Protector
Pilgrim
Pulse of life
Patient God

Quickener
Questioner

Rock
Reaper
Refuge of my love
Root
Rescuer

Summoner of the stars
Son of Mary
Scatterer
Strong God
Sustainer of the universe

Teller of tales
Traveller
Touchstone of truth
Treasure

Vibrant God
Voice of glory

Warm, wise God
Weaver
Warden of heaven
Wellspring of grace
Wonder of wonders

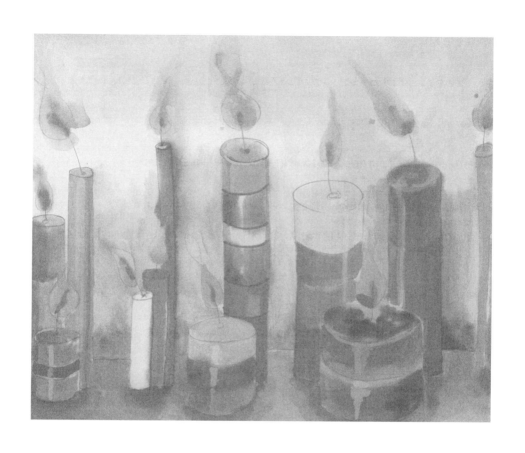

ADVENT CRIES –
A WRITING WORKSHOP
(for groups)

ADVENT CRIES –
A WRITING WORKSHOP (FOR GROUPS)

Optimum size: 12 to 15 people
Time: 75 or 85 minutes
Aim: to encourage participants to write and share Advent cries

For this workshop you will need:

☆ Words and music for *O Come, O Come, Emmanuel*
☆ Pencils
☆ Paper
☆ Flip chart and pens
☆ (Optional: pictures, photos, drawings portraying God at work – Christmas cards, line drawings from *The Good News Bible*, news pictures, copies of paintings)
☆ Bibles and concordances

FORMAT:

Sing/play

Sing or play: *O Come, O Come, Emmanuel*

List the names

Ask people to list the names given to God in each verse of *O Come, O Come,*

Emmanuel (Emmanuel, Branch of Jesse, Dayspring, Key of David, Adonai/Ruler of the House of Israel). List the names on the flip chart.

History

Talk about the history and context of the Advent cries (see pages 54–56).

Structure

Look at the structure of an Advent cry:

☆ O Title (of God or the Messiah)
☆ This is how you act
☆ Come and act in us and in our world

Look at this structure in two Advent cries.

Pictures and names

Either: In small groups, look at pictures/photos/drawings which portray God at work and write a list of names/titles for God suggested by these pictures.

And/or: In small groups, take a section of the alphabet each, A-D, E-H, etc, and make lists of names/titles for God beginning with these letters.

List of names

Write the names on the flip chart.

Writing

Write an Advent cry (alone, with a partner?).

Sharing

Share what you've written

Singing and praying

Sing or play *O Come, O Come, Emmanuel* and read out your prayers between the verses, with everyone saying *Amen* to each prayer.

An additional activity might be making posters or banners on which to write the Advent cries that have been created in the workshop.

ACTIVITIES	MINUTES
Sing/play *O Come, O Come, Emmanuel*	5
List names on the flip chart	5
History and context of the Advent cries	10
Look at the structure of the Advent cries	5
EITHER Pictures and names in small groups	10
AND/OR Alphabetical names in small groups	10
Look at the list of names (flip chart?)	5
Writing Advent cries	15
Sharing what has been written	10
Song and prayers	10
TOTAL TIME	75 or 85

FOR YOUR OWN ADVENT CRIES ...

FOR YOUR OWN ADVENT CRIES ...

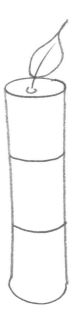

FOR YOUR OWN ADVENT CRIES ...

ADVENT CRIES –
A POSTER/BANNER
WORKSHOP

ADVENT CRIES –
A POSTER/BANNER WORKSHOP

Optimum size: 12 to 20
Time: 85 minutes
Aim: to create posters and/or banners relating to the Advent antiphons

For this workshop you will need:

☆ A range of art materials, e.g. poster paints, finger paints, watercolours, fluorescent paints in squeezy bottles, glitter, collage material, glue, a variety of brushes, clay, wire, cardboard, paper, scissors, felt pens, pencils
☆ Paper or thin card as a base for posters; hessian or another strong material of one colour as a base for banners
☆ Words and music for *O Come, O Come, Emmanuel*
☆ Bibles and concordances

FORMAT:

Sing/play

Sing or play *O Come, O Come, Emmanuel*

History

Talk about the history and context of the Advent cries (see pages 54–56)

O Wisdom

Look at the traditional cry for the 17th December – O Wisdom (see pages 58–59).

Read the biblical and literary references (see pages 57–71).

Think about symbols that could be used to portray wisdom.

Symbols

In small groups, look briefly at the other six cries (pages 60–71) and suggest symbols.

Make a list.

Art materials

Introduce a range of art materials.

Decide who would like to work on which cry.

Creating

Create posters/banners of the Advent cries:

☆ The posters could be entirely pictorial.
☆ A phrase from the Advent cry could be included in the poster.
☆ Text could be written on a separate label to accompany the poster.

Sharing

Look at the posters/banners and talk about them.

Singing

Sing *O Come, O Come, Emmanuel.*

The posters/banners could be taken home or displayed all together somewhere.

ACTIVITIES	MINUTES
Sing or play *O Come, O Come, Emmanuel*	5
History and context of the Advent cries	10
Look at the cry *O Wisdom*	10
In groups, look at other cries. Suggest symbols	10
Look at the art materials available	5
Create posters/banners	30
Look at and talk about each other's work	10
Sing or play *O Come, O Come, Emmanuel*	5
TOTAL TIME	85

ADVENT CRIES –
AN ALL-AGE WORKSHOP

ADVENT CRIES –
AN ALL-AGE WORKSHOP

Number: variable
Time: 70 minutes
Aim: to experience the Advent antiphons in an all-age setting, using song, drama, discussion, art and craft

For this workshop you will need:

☆ 4 well-briefed group leaders (see Activities section)
☆ Someone to lead the singing
☆ Someone to act out names we use to describe God
☆ A wide range of art materials – paint in squeezy bottles, felt pens (lots), pencils, paintbrushes, finger paints, glue, glitter, thin card, scissors, magazines to cut up for collages, pipe cleaners, cloth, modelling clay, coloured paper, drawing paper, etc.
☆ Mobiles from which to hang the pictures and sayings created in the workshop and/or poster paper or banners on which to display the pictures and sayings and/or string on which to hang the pictures/sayings. (See NB p.97)
☆ Pictures of keys and/or templates of keys
☆ List of people in Jesus's family tree (Matthew 1:1–17 and Luke 3:23–28) and ideas for pictures, e.g. Noah's ark, Jacob's ladder, a harp for David, corn for Ruth, a temple for Solomon.
☆ Pictures and/or templates of moons, planets, stars, spaceships
☆ A few starter ideas for wise sayings, e.g. 'Look before you leap'.

NB: The pictures/sayings (the keys, family tree pictures, stars, planets and wise sayings) that are later created in the groups can be displayed in a number of ways:

☆ Hung on mobiles (the keys, etc need to be made two-sided)
☆ Pasted onto posters or glued onto banners
☆ Hung on strings strung across the room (the keys, etc need to be made two-sided)
☆ Taken home and hung up somewhere as a reminder of the day

FORMAT:

Song: *Advent Waiting* (see p.101)

Talk about names and nicknames

Nicknames are names that describe what someone is like – the job they do, the place they live. (Bob the Builder, Angelina Ballerina …)

5 minutes in small groups

Does anyone in your family/school/workplace have a nickname?

Is it a good one? (Nicknames can be cruel as well as kind.)

Names for God

Can you think of some names we call God, use to describe God?

Someone could act out some well-known names and get people guessing! (Shepherd, King, Father ...)

The Advent cries

The people who wrote the prayers we call the Advent cries used a variety of names and titles for God. The names they chose come from the Bible. They are names that describe the hoped-for Messiah, and that we sometimes use when we talk about Jesus.

Wisdom
Key of David
Ruler of Israel
Root of Jesse
King of the nations
Dayspring/Morning star
Emmanuel

(Choose how much detail you want to go into here. If young children are part of the workshop, keep it to a minimum.)

Activities for four groups:

(Each group has a group leader)

1. KEY OF DAVID

Look at keys in your pockets – what do you use them for?
Have you ever lost a key? Tell each other what happened?

Make some keys (large and small) from the art materials.

2. ROOT OF JESSE

Explain what a family tree is.
Draw some simple family trees for members of the group (siblings, parents, grandparents). Be sensitive to painful individual family histories. (This section can be omitted.)
Talk about Jesus's family tree.
Draw some pictures relating to people in Jesus's family tree: a garden for Adam and Eve, Noah's ark, Jacob's ladder, a harp for David, corn for Ruth, a temple for Solomon …

3. DAYSPRING/MORNING STAR

Talk about the stars and the planets.
Who has seen the sunrise?
In the Christmas story, who followed a star? Where did it lead them?

Make stars, planets, moons, spaceships and a sun from the art materials.

4. WISDOM

What does it mean to be wise?
Talk about some wise people, old and young.
Think of six or more wise sayings or proverbs.

Use the art materials to illustrate your wise sayings. Draw patterns around them; create pictures/cartoons to illustrate them.

Display your art work

Look at each other's creativity

Song: *Advent Waiting* (see opposite) or a familiar Advent or Christmas carol

ACTIVITIES	MINUTES
Song: *Advent Waiting*	5
Names and nicknames	5
In small groups	5
Names for God	5
Advent cries	5
Activities in groups	25
Look at each other's creativity	5
Song	5
TOTAL TIME	70 (and then clear up!)

Song: Advent Waiting

Tune: *Frère Jacques*

(Each line could be sung by a song-leader then repeated by everyone. You could move round the room to sing verses, standing near the symbols mentioned in each verse.)

1. Advent waiting
   Advent sighs
   Long nights of December
   Advent cries

2. God is holy
   God is wise
   Advent cries of wisdom
   Fill the skies

3. Roots and branches
   Family trees
   Jesus, Mary, Joseph,
   Adam and Eve

4. Opening windows
   David's Key
   Opening doors and padlocks
   Setting free

5. Bright red sunrise
   Morning star
   Scattering the darkness
   Near and far

6. Advent waiting
   Advent sighs
   Short days of December
   Advent cries.

NOTES

NOTES

NOTES

NOTES

THE IONA COMMUNITY IS:

- An ecumenical movement of men and women from different walks of life and different traditions in the Christian church
- Committed to the gospel of Jesus Christ, and to following where that leads, even into the unknown
- Engaged together, and with people of goodwill across the world, in acting, reflecting and praying for justice, peace and the integrity of creation
- Convinced that the inclusive community we seek must be embodied in the community we practise

Together with our staff, we are responsible for:

- Our islands residential centres of Iona Abbey, the MacLeod Centre on Iona, and Camas Adventure Centre on the Ross of Mull

and in Glasgow:

- The administration of the Community
- Our work with young people
- Our publishing house, Wild Goose Publications
- Our association in the revitalising of worship with the Wild Goose Resource Group

The Iona Community was founded in Glasgow in 1938 by George MacLeod, minister, visionary and prophetic witness for peace, in the context of the poverty and despair of the Depression. Its original task of rebuilding the monastic ruins of Iona Abbey became a sign of hopeful rebuilding of community in Scotland and beyond. Today, we are about 250 Members, mostly in Britain, and 1500 Associate Members, with 1400 Friends worldwide. Together and apart, 'we follow the light we have, and pray for more light'.

For information on the Iona Community contact:
The Iona Community, Fourth Floor, Savoy House, 140 Sauchiehall Street,
Glasgow G2 3DH, UK. Phone: 0141 332 6343
e-mail: ionacomm@gla.iona.org.uk; web: www.iona.org.uk

For enquiries about visiting Iona, please contact:
Iona Abbey, Isle of Iona, Argyll PA76 6SN, UK. Phone: 01681 700404
e-mail: ionacomm@iona.org.uk

ALSO FROM WILD GOOSE PUBLICATIONS

A Book of Blessings
... and how to write your own
Ruth Burgess

This Wild Goose best-seller is a collection of blessings for the people, sadnesses, artefacts, special occasions and journeys of our lives. It also explores the tradition of blessings, including biblical and Celtic, and offers ideas and resources to encourage readers to write blessings of their own, with suggestions for how to organise a blessings workshop.

ISBN 1 901557 48 0

Friends and Enemies
A book of short prayers & some ways to write your own
Ruth Burgess

A collection of prayers about relationships and the particular moments and places of our daily lives. They convey wisdom and humour, while some contain strong thoughts and words. 'Saying what we mean to God,' writes Ruth Burgess, 'is more honest than tiptoeing around the issues and concerns we find disturbing or difficult. To write with integrity is to write within the traditions of the writers of the psalms.' *Friends and Enemies* is offered as a resource for personal prayer and public worship, and as an encouragement to both individuals and congregations to be creative and courageous in their prayers. Includes three prayer-writing workshops.

ISBN 1 901557 78 2

Eggs & Ashes
Practical and liturgical resources for Lent and Holy Week
Ruth Burgess & Chris Polhill

Suitable for group worship or personal reflection, and with material for Shrove Tuesday, Ash Wednesday, Mothering Sunday, Palm Sunday and Holy Week, this is a collection to accompany readers through Lent and Easter for many years. Includes a Lent discipline for those who care about the environment, liturgies, responses, prayers, poems, reflections, meditations, stories, stations of the cross, sermons, monologues and songs, with some all-age resources – written by Iona Community members, associates, friends and others.

ISBN 1 901557 87 1

Praying for the Dawn
A resource book for the ministry of healing
Ruth Burgess & Kathy Galloway

A compilation of material from several writers with strong emphasis on liturgies and resources for healing services. Includes a section on how to introduce healing services to those who may not be familiar with them, and suggestions for starting group discussions about healing. The book is rounded off by a section of worship resources – prayers, responses, litanies, poems, meditations and blessings.

ISBN 1 901557 26 X